If Seasons Were Kingdoms

Margaret Koger

Fernwood
PRESS

If Seasons Were Kingdoms

©2024 by Margaret Koger

Fernwood Press
Newberg, Oregon
www.fernwoodpress.com

Printed in the United States of America

Cover and page design: Mareesa Fawver Moss
Cover photo by Eric Muhr
Author photo by Betty Rodgers

ISBN 978-1-59498-128-9

If Seasons Were Kingdoms is a beautiful, riddling book. Enriched with mythological, classical allusions and scientific terminology, Margaret Koger's poems often begin with simple, sight-specific images or scenes from nature. The poet then expands these images into broader, more global observations. The eerie cry of a wild swan reminds the poet that she lives "by naming days." She also uses unexpected verbs to flesh out her nature imagery: "Spring roots knuckle the earth," "A glassy lake / spits leaping cutthroat," "Pollen scents clamor," "Snow skiffs on branches," and "Wind . . . never forgets my name." The seasons culminate in the final question of the book: "Does anyone hear the owl's voice, or yours / or mine, speaking of our ages and what / we've learned or have yet to do / before crossing into moonlight?" Margaret Koger hears the owl's voice, the river's, the salmon's, and the mountain's. Her poems speak their words.

BARBARA OLIC-HAMILTON writes reviews for *BookWomen: A Reader's Community for Those Who Love Women's Words* as well as her own accomplished fiction, memoir, and poetry

In *If Seasons Were Kingdoms*, we have a speaker who ventures forth among the robins and the swans, the killdeer and the finches, the avocets and the herons, and reports back to us, the fortunate readers, on "what my forefathers didn't know": this close communion, this vision of the earth as "a prospectus for seeds," everywhere the possibility of further fecundities. There's more than a bit of the Rilkean imperative here—You must change your life—but what calls us to it in *If Seasons Were Kingdoms* is not the archaic but the immediate: "How deer hold/ barely breathing," the poet says, and follows this with "See? Who are you?" It's a question, the poet asserts—and I believe her—that we have to leave our houses to answer.

KERRI WEBSTER is the Idaho Writer-in-Residence for 2024–2025 and the author of four books of poetry: *Lapis, The Trailhead, Grand & Arsenal,* and *We Do Not Eat Our Hearts Alone*

In Margaret Koger's *If Seasons Were Kingdoms*, the poet leads us on a journey riddled with puzzles, on a search for the narrator. Loss, time, space, need, nature, birds, birds in flight, scenes of nature pure and simple and profound, more need, much need, a journey, a fox, deer and more deer, a narrator's intimate mating with nature. Written, as the poetry says, in a "Braille of clean air."

KEN RODGERS is the author of *The Gods of Angkor Wat*, a poet, and co-director of the award-winning documentaries: *Bravo!*, *Common Men, Uncommon Valor*, and *I Married the War*

Many thanks to Grove Koger, whose close readings of these poems immeasurably helped them land on their feet. Many thanks as well for the endless assistance of the Whittenberger Writing Group—Jim, Barb, Lola, Gaymon, and Tony—and members of Poetry in the City of Trees. Thanks also to the *Idaho Writers Update*, the Idaho Writers Guild, and others in the Boise Valley community who encouraged me throughout.

Contents

Acknowledgments

Avocet: A Journal of Nature Poems. "Glisten," previously "At the Cabin on Clear Creek," 2009. "Sunset at Hell Roaring Lake," Summer 2010; reprinted in *Awake in the World* 2, Riverfeet Press, 2019.

Cirque. "May One," 2024.

Deep Wild. "Sharing Tarn Water," 3, 2021.

Forbidden Peak Press. "The Bears of Redfish Lake," 1st Place, 1st Summer Poetry Contest, 2019.

Friends of Acadia Journal. "Little Sturgeon," 2nd Place, 2012 Poetry Contest, 17, no. 2, Summer 2012.

Gravitas. "Nine Ways of Inhaling Night," 19, no. 1, 2020.

Heron Clan. "Lament of the Pando Aspen," 8, 2021.

Kudzu Review. "Coda of the Accidental Clown," 1, no. 1, Winter Solstice 2011.

The Limberlost Review: A Literary Journal of the Mountain West. "Drink Starlight" and "The Hike," 2021.

MacQueen's Quinterly. "Winter Wings" and "Ream of Sky," Jan. 2024.

Mocking Bird Review. "Night Rain," Feb. 2020.

Mouse Tale Press. "A Simple Gift," previously "Round Valley Canon," March 2012; "Mouse Tale," Apr. 2012; "Spotted Fawn," May 2012.

Pagan Friends. "Walking down Sunday Roads," 2011.

Parks and Points. "The Desire" is based on "Discovery in the Nature Center," 8, Apr. 24, 2021.

Ponder Savant. "First Light at Dagger Falls," "The Reservoir: The Return," and "River Therapy," May 2020.

Subjectiv [sic]. "Ghost of a Robin" and "The Field Hungers," no. 3, Fall 2020.

Tiny Seed Literary Journal. "Corn Lilies" and "In the Forest," previously "Spring in the Forest near Stanley," Winter 2019.

Writers in the Attic: The Cabin. *[Animal]* "Call of the Wild Swan" and "How Sweet the Sparrow's Song," 2015; *[Game]* "Hunting Pheasant," 2017; and *[Song]* "Song of the Northern Honeysuckle," 2018.

I. The Stir

I am yours   come from shadows clutched   by sheer white drifts
a changeling   astir in soaked seedbeds   as husks rot   seedlings
swell   bulbs blossom   warm winds   coddle thawing limbs
pummeled by rain

Who am I?

Ghost of a Robin

Let's call her Lucy—

On the skinniest branch
of a paper birch
where slender limbs spear the sky
a robin was

On the same day leaf buds
pulled back into their bracts
having tasted acid air
retreating from hard knocks
coming on from a diamond-glint summer

Only now suffering   what past   what future
will be   will be

As if by plan the ghost of yesterday's robin
lingers on the skinniest branch
toes clamped

I weave a needle into the gauze of day
and pluck it out again

Don't you see? she said,
We all come from there—
stardust

Live Like You Mean It

In spring

Trees lean away from high winds
Roots discuss the need for clinging

Snowmelt flashes in white cascades
Rivers tumble, then flatten

Squirrels unearth the last walnuts
from fall caches

Migrating flocks swoop into trees
feathers primed for mating flurries

Nesting's of primary concern

I need a new life

Call of the Wild Swan

At dawn an eerie cry unravels

      from the long neck of a wild swan
          reminds me I live by naming days—
               Sunday, Monday, spending a sigh here
               a tremble there   my calendar
                   shielding me as I try not to remember
               the pure timbre of swans trumpeting
         epic cycles into a world meant to last
      larger and longer than I   songs repeating
how I am truly nothing   if not to hear this call.

The Field

If seasons were kingdoms
I'd roll   acres and acres of earth
a prospectus for seeds   welcome
their slow push   fertile rhymes
inviting the souls of hawks
the *kill-kill* cry of killdeer
wing-stuttered—a fox's *yapyap*.

If seasons were kingdoms
I'd bed the maiden breezes
listen for their whispers
sweets for furrows
sweets for bearded shoots
row after row   in me and of me
my soil   hungry to confer.

I'd stretch beneath sky's giddy blue,
drink droplets from sprinklers
coddle earthworms and beetles
as my fellows   fox and hawk feast
by tooth and talon

I'd hunger only for the braille of clean air
sun warmed   slow summers
my greens to flourish   burst forth
until thick rime   clings of snow
spelled harvest   the given
          you'd gather.

Spring Equinox

Yesterday almost—
Now the sun halves the earth
Birds in trees fluster

Hailstones drum our ground
Thunder roars as lightning strikes
Whites of my wide eyes

Snow banks around the trees
Clearing skies shadow long limbs
Snug of squirrel nest

Cottonwoods float seeds
White curtains billow and blow
Where have you gone?

Creeping into mind
Fog saunters into my rhyme
Clouds my hazel eye

Sunlight blues the sky
Buds unfold into blossom
Bees please my honey

Corn Lilies on Galena Summit

Melting snow reveals green shoots
lily namesakes for tall stalks of cereal crops
whose kernels feed humans and livestock.

Some long-ago pollen crossing
by a mischievous wind   or a silly bee
mixed maize and lilies   sacred flowers

storied harbingers of death.
I too am hybrid   foolish in my concern
over mind   or matter   but at this summit

I reconcile if not to spring's promise
then to sturdy lilies' stems piercing snow
coupling this cogent   pair lily and me

but I   I am the one who waits.

Night Rain

A damp lung
the forest
inhales   filling the tent
soaking me to wake.

The storm
spending its last silver
buys absolute
silence.

The Bears of Redfish Lake

I

Near the campgrounds at Redfish
Milky Way bear-stars wink broadly
from the still water of the lake.

A brown sow waits to stir at dawn
when light filters into her cave and rouses
hunger to its plaintive outcry.

She'll take her cubs to a culvert where
ants swarm their paws as they break
the night's fast   slurp formic acid.

On to a downfall   a rotted log harbor
where white grubs   wriggle to escape
the cubs' salivating tongues.

The risen sow will guide her cubs
to dig   their soft claws hardened now
rip the ground   digging out tubers.

2.

Soon there will be mice and voles
meaty challenges to untested teeth
tearing open fur skin red-flesh.

In a month she'll lead them
sashaying uphill for berry picking
when huckleberries purple to sweet.

Her spirit   Big Bear of the Micmac
hunted by Cherokee   Moose Bird
Robin stained red by a bear's blood.

3

Add Callisto   once a Roman maiden
then Juno's groundling sow   so debased
the mighty Jupiter pitied her *and* her son

—snatched them through the air

(said Ovid)

in whirlwinds up to heaven and fix'd them there.

Frigid points of fire   Ursa Major   Ursa Minor
never to dip below the north horizon
never a freshening drink or a cool bath.

Nights inside the dark mantle of her cave
the sow cuddles her dreaming cubs
falling asleep as campers drink stars
                        from solar dippers.

Finding Your Way

On a clear night   climb thirsty
follow a winding trail to an alpine lake
stop and gaze up until you find Ursa Minor
her dipper forever circles north   lifts

your desire   from slippery logs   outlet to inlet
into streamlet narrows   until you

slake your   star light   star bright   thirst.
Sail clean to the pole star   steady light
fading   only when Venus sparks the dawn.

II. Thumbs of Bright Colors

I invite you   bask in sunny heat   as thumbs of bright colors   thrust up
on rings of hot days   sap-formed buds   fill to fruited globes
succulent ears kernel   straw necks bend in praise   my loins bear

Who am I?

May One

magnolia buds drip dew   finches startle
male merganser tuxedos fade to brown
bald eagle's white pierces gray skies

I can breathe

First Light at Dagger Falls

Follow me into the wilderness
watch the Chinook leap whitewater
as dawn spreads color on canyon walls
sun silvers the backs of salmon below

there! a female   whips above the rapids
hangs a moment, twists before falling
her pulse a drum to overtake the flow
the coax of her blush-red roe seeks
the streambed where she hatched   a smolt
such as her eggs will become

now! the male bursts from the froth   leaps
fighting to follow   miles to go into shallows
where they'll spawn   milt, eggs, gametes
as earth's magnetic pulse   imprints

inspiring me   my heart in flight
soars   to perch in a ponderosa   where
I'm avian   soon   kited on cliff winds
peering down into pines soughed

in desire   my pulse beats   as I wait
for an updraft   to carry me a lover
a sturdy male   ready to find a redd.

The Bird a Nest

The bird a nest, the spider a web, man friendship.
—*William Blake*

1

Killdeer at my feet—

a pair of birds
scraping dry soil for room
to lay eggs raise hatchlings.
If you're too close *awk awk awk*
then a limp wing hanging
tail feathers drag in pretense
as if you were a fox
to be lured away
leave our nest
begone.

2

I see white webs a spider—

silent as it spit-weaves sheets of lacy
canopy on the tips of evergreen boughs
white dresses for prickly needles,
its eight eyes fixed body tense
arms itching to capture
the hapless fly.

3
The trees my friends—

my friends the trees
I touch bark stately oaks
trunks a ring fuller each year
limbs stretching high and higher
while our candles burn low and lower
under the shade of our fellows
as killdeer hatchlings
eye the sky.

Little Sturgeon

As you pass under this
exoskeletal span of bridge,
I note your snout-nosed slide
wide-spread fins like hands
seven-foot wavy-tailed torso
just a homely fish-puppy.

And I wonder as you glide
above mud's cloudy limit
do you observe earth's crust
holding the pond water up?
As a self-appointed inspector
of slime do you detect how
sprinkler rain rotates evenly
plopping your sky with circles?

Scutes support and protect you
but as for me each yearly cycle
sloughs off my oldest cells
replacements itching to find
a caesura of gravity

                              or time

for some prescient guarantee
against these passing decades
so sturdily forcing me down.

Oh little sturgeon swim widely
linger a hundred years or more
buoyed by your isinglass bladder
over the pond's low pastures
aswirl in your watery slant

                    long after I pass by.

In the Forest

Sapling roots knuckle the earth
as green shoots summon visions
and fresh buds line raw creeks.
Water spirits nurture torrents
white crescendos flooding
down from alpine heights.

Loggers rapped by lusty thumps
of ruffed grouse males courting.
Men stirred by sweet camas scents
the stippled ooze of raw pitch.
Men shouldering heavy chainsaws
tools revved and roaring to bite.

Stag elk bugle and rut as men
head into the forest; their ears
longing to hear *timber!* feet ready
to leap aside as giant yellow pines
crash down around them.

Rings marking years of growth
sliced; open arteriole flows bleed.
Logs chained and hoisted on trucks;
logs for lumber to renew the world.

Loggers muscling one tree at a time.
Men alive with pitch, burnt oil, dirt.

Ream of Sky

Who will measure
      the ream of sky
            wherein the heron
has yet to fly?

Sharing Tarn Water

Find a spring and settle
    welcome the damp
        mossy air   clean smell

The pool mirrors your face
    your elbows bend
        as you inhale—

Yes go on settle
    on palms and knees
        leaning forward

Your face disappears
    as cool water surrounds
        lips mouth chin

You must sip gently
    savor the clear liquid
        careful not to breathe

    only swallow
        swallow
            swallow—

Then rise step back slowly
    wipe your chin
        walk away—

Glance over your shoulder
    see a doe stepping forward
        it's her turn

The Glisten

At the cabin on Clear Creek
over the low flame of a Coleman
I boiled beet sugar water
poured cooled syrup into a feeder
hung the dripping red vessel
from a nail on the cabin eaves.

I offered this sticky imitation   Cinquefoil
Scarlet Gilia   Crimson Columbine.

I waited   waited   under the blazing sun
standing in drought-bitten cheatgrass.

Suddenly   *buzz* and *whirr*
          zig and zag of weighty air   ripped open.

Long-tongued   ruby-throated Calliope
          flashed a green silver purple glisten

barely paused to sup   then darted—

the sweet red pretender to nectar   taken
the hummer   for a moment   mine.

The Reservoir

One by one shore birds take wing   avocets   a gray heron
stick-feet tucked   wings spread   safely away.

Our boat rises   slaps down   bucking the wakes of speedsters.
We round the curve   and slow   near Robie Creek dock.

The inlet eye shines   tempts children   to burst from cars
race barefoot across concrete   their tangled voices   echo

days we recall   to wade and splash   sparkle into rainbows.

The Spotted Fawn

I see you snuggled there
    spine curled damply inward
        amid wild strawberry leaves
            taut berry stems spiky grass.
Two rows of airy white chevrons
    swell down your smooth flanks
        trail into a spunky white tail.

Dew on your wet black nose
liquid of your wet brown eyes.

Who tore aside your cozy glen
    sheltering leaves ripped apart
        exposing you to the camera eye
            casting a spell on your baby spots?

A prize for humans who stop time
    so we can dream over an image
        trace a pretty picture on paper

with fingers longing to touch.

Sunset at Hell Roaring Lake

A glassy lake spits
leaping cutthroat
arcs of silver
angles of sharp fins
spiraling out of water
in frenzied flight.

Twisting as arrows
passing through
Alice's mirror
opening one universe
into another
—water air water.

A furious rush
hungry to outrun darkness
as one by one
tiny flies succumb
disappear in the mouths
of fish before night
swallows the fish
swallows the fly.

The Hike

Here in the Great Basin
I stand at the foot of Wheeler Peak
where ancient bristlecones survive
sky-high on glacial moraines
      my feet aching from the climb

fingers tracing striated limbs
solid beneath a blazing sun
where the dense wood shuns
insects, fungi, rot, fires, disease
and sub-zero nights

      killers all for me—

minor gods who grow no rings
in years of extreme weather
mates to the howling wind
their claw-like scales on cones
ready to guard seeds for saplings
to live another five thousand years.

How Sweet the Sparrow Sings

A girl who holds the calls of birds so dear
      sits waiting for the Sunday rhymes to clear.

She hears no joy in four-four anthem rhyming
      prays a yellow warbler's *zuzzy* buzzing.

A meadowlark's stout yellow open throat
      will spell an honest timbre to each note.

A vireo's *cheerio chireep* lifts higher
      spare melodies of soul she so desires.

So when the pushy hymns are finally done
      she'll smile and bow her head and quickly run

to rest beneath her friends of ash and alder
      to cache a sparrow's *cheep cheep t-reeeer*!

III. Bringing in the Sheaves

If you come   I ride the cusp   sword arm ready to slay
hunger's gaunt heart   his body bruised   tethered sheaves
of golden hue   burdens sweet to carry   with humble mien
obedient axe soon splitting   wood to fuel hearth fires

Who am I?

A Simple Gift

'Tis the gift to be simple, 'tis the gift to be free.
—Shaker Song

Meeting you by chance
I see Round Valley again.

Walk down the damp
meadow pathways
unwinds our sad story.

Notes of lavender lupine
straighten my spine
as pain   betrayal lift.

High in the pure flute
of shooting stars
above quartets of cowslip

I listen to peace play.
Pine and wind combine
to serenade me free.

I want to reach out
pry open the dry shell
around your heart

turn you round and round
'til you turn out right.

Make That Terra Firma

Geared up for a challenge
twisting up the asphalt strip.
Going to the Sun in Montana
sniffing the engine's sweat of hot oil
tires straining to grind upward
conquering the glacier's cut
—6,646 feet into the sky.

Whelming over Donner Pass
chains gripping the slick
icy road as cagey winds paw
itching to spin us into snow banks
where once the party ended
—7,056 feet above the sea.

Revving engines up the Alcan
hell bent for beyond the Yukon
—over 1,300 miles of wilderness.

Pushing past the altars of humdrum
free to conquer miles and miles
sitting astride wheels bought
and paid for—our pride—setting
the purchase of the land aside
we trek—hither and yon
as if to overcome the earth.

The Way

Holding my breath
in the hollow of my chest
where stale air lingers
lungs wait to expand.

The way
fall follows the fleeing sun
winter wraps a chill around
grass greens in the spring.
The way
mountain crags crumble
rivers rendezvous
tides follow the moon.

How deer hold
barely breathing.
See? Who are you?
How dogs bark
warning intruders
saving our bodies
not saving our lives.
How Mama's smile
lit her face and mine.

The way
I knock on wood, but
can't find my other shoe.

The Interlude

I walk a sunny meadow
        where carpets of spongy grass
                tempt me to settle in

but pollen scents clamor
        jangled at bees' antennae
                blossom clusters nod and sway
                        in yellow swatches and blue and white

polka dots cluttering in calico patches while
        tangled flower stems stitch themselves
                into grasping quilts
                        where roots cut into
clumps of sodden soil
        threaded by millions
                of sprouting seeds
                        pushing, needling up
chanting *me, me*—

Not the meadow then; I head onward
        to the Idaho high desert sweeps
of solitary air, to catch my breath
                        surrounded by boundless vistas

a few sego lilies nodding at my feet
        wind that wraps the earth in airy arms
                thermals the vultures' carrion flight
                        wind that never forgets *my name.*

To Die For

Exploring a trail
circling a mountain lake—
at the inlet I discovered

two rare orchids   eyes peering at me
moccasin-chins framed by spirals
red sepal-braids,   bold yellow

lady slipper mouths invited me to bumble
if I bee, to zoom into a golden tunnel
stroll on neon green.

Miles of pines   in green surround
spoke to each other of survival—
only one coddling brilliance.

I was young   and alone
unacquainted with wilderness
bereft of tooth and claw.

Struck with wonder, I pinched
two blossoms   scalped from stems
weeping xylem tears   orchid

blood oozing to the forest floor.
I slipped them into my pack
assassination complete.

In camp   lady slipper chins
sepal braids wilted   eyes closed.
I hurried their sad faces

onto white paper
pressed them in a poetry book
to dry, ready to haunt me

for years to come.

Drink Starlight

Light pours down the Big Dipper
Ursa Major. Stars of the great
she-bear's flank trace the bowl
stars of the dipper's handle ready

to your command as you come
thirsty through the night to the well
grasping the long-handled dipper
from the nail beside the cistern.

Hold the cup beneath the spout
lever the pump arm up down
and as the cold water gushes
catch a splash before the rest
pools in the pail.

Raise the dipper to your lips
drink starlight, clean and spare.

Peer into the pail below
starlight, crystal white:
the bear stars' rippling kiss.

Hunting Pheasant

Yes   but judge not until you've sat in the truck
cuddled an earlier kill   a warm ring-neck
rooster in your lap

you've loved the jeweled feathers   stroked
the emerald sheen beside the white neck ring
beauties beyond the peacock's lofty elegance.

You wait until the men and dogs emerge
from yellowed stalks in fields as ripe as
this cumulus corn-fed bountiful day

wait to head home with a lapful of pheasant
promising tender breast-meat at table.

The Sun Glides Away

Yesterday's warm flow
cools to chill river ripples
Swimsuits put away

Zinnia colors zing
A brilliant moon stalks the sky
Shine baby shine on

Acorns fall *plop plop*
Squirrels hustle and bustle
hiding winter fare

Hummingbirds depart
Geese vee south in symmetry
Will my love go too?

When the m-m-m-moon shines
over the c-c-c cowshed
I'll be waiting—

Cold clear nights no wind
Hoar frost ruptures stems let go
Gold leaves swirl to earth

The Desire

I walk to the Nature Center
where I see a fuzzy round
something on a wild rose
a *Rosa acicularis* with canes
stung by *Diplolepis rosea*
cynipid wasps providing
homes for their stout larvae.

And because chemicals fail
against these hardy insects
you must wait for the leaves
to shrivel and fall away
wear gloves pluck them out.

Or in the spring thirty forty
full-grown wasps will emerge
aching to lay more eggs breed
on the stems of hapless roses.

But this is a native plant garden
where I will not stand as savior
to roses thriving even as the virus
stings my every desire to touch.

Zephyr Day +

On the river walk
the day arrives
sun full on
sky robin blue
scatters of calm wind
chatter the trees
—it's here.

—

September, October
leaves' chlorophyl fades
flares of caroten gold
dazzles of antho red
royals of tannin brown
sun circles southerly
—holding, like breath.

x

Branches push
leaves abscised
by corky winter coats
leaves unleaving
—unique relief.

+

Scatters of calm zephyrs
kiss the bark as limbs
twitch and tingle release
glories of leaves
—hearts instead of hands.

x
Brown skirt-wrapped
trunks hum finales
to another year's ring
—when I'll be older.

=
November a zephyr
days' reckoning
and yet more leaves
cling here there
the weight of fall
—still on my shoulders.

IV. Nodding Off

Your shawl? I slumber deep   in weary dark   eyes fiercely closed
feigned rest   my dank locks lengthen   curls of withering blasts
whip to grassy rooftops   bare-bent forest branches   snare unwary
walkers   felling foolish travelers

Who am I?

Mouse Tale

Dead center in the glare of headlights I see a tiny gray flurry turn into a silver mouse. She slides round and round, trapped on a patch of black ice, while my tires roll forward like aliens, driven by the fire in the engine. It hums in rhythmic power. Anywhere the tires touch the mouse, she will die.

I wonder what called her out of her tiny hole before dawn. To find food, I imagine, her store of seeds empty, milk too scant for hungry pups. Was she tempted by curiosity or joy? Is dawn a time of renewal for her too? Or she may be old, confused, and found herself at risk.

Here the ice, traffic, danger. I see her again in my mirror, still spinning. Will the next car spare her? The next? A tiny twirler unable to grip the ice, held captive by gravity and cold, a speck in the galaxy, infinitesimal in an expanding universe. Round and round she whirls, once and forever in my memory. What is it this one mouse offers?

Mouse Tale Whiteout

Dead center   I see a tiny gray flurry

                                         trapped on a

patch of black ice

                                              Anywhere

the tires touch   she will die.

I wonder what called her out

                                         milk too scant

     hungry pups   dawn
a time of renewal   she may be old, confused

          ice, traffic, danger   mirror, still
spinning
unable   captive

                    expanding universe. Round and

round   in my memory

     one mouse

Nine Ways of Inhaling Night

Look to the stars! Look, look up at the skies!
—Gerard Manley Hopkins

Moonlight

Pour moonlight in a goblet
        sip its bare-knuckle distillation
                veil of unrivaled white

Hydra

Cling to Hydra's coil with Corvus crow
        staccato *caw caw* loves me
                loves me not

Phoenix

Strike a chord in a Phoenix flight
        stir flame into its curvy tail
                sing ashes to ashes

Ariadne

Color your sails Corona Borealis
        gold of Ariadne's crown
                its jeweled eye blinking

Orion

Hitch a ride on Orion's slide
        stream flares of stardust fire
                burn baby burn

Pulsars

Paraphrase Crab Nebula with
       pulsars beating in your veins
              nova nova supernova

Columba

Lash your heart to Columba's ring
       soar above the darkened flood
              Noah disappears at sunrise

Cygnus

Free a swan to fly before dawn
       Cygnus—a flurry of feathers
              Leda slung aloft

Selene

Gaze to the east at twilight
       inhale the rise of a crescent moon
              flash your diamond eyes

Coda of the Accidental Clown

Driving down Highway 21 before sunrise
just above Lucky Peak Dam I see shadows
deer whose dark limbs rend the fog.

A herd flows over slick asphalt
a dark line leaps the rails one by one
until this doe stares into my headlights.

A nick of the fender turns her
flesh and bone marrow and hide.
Ripped from her morning circuit
she sails a tumbling head-over-hooves clown
smearing red smiles on my windshield.

A crowd gathers men pull her aside
someone will harvest the meat they say.
I scarcely hear this soothing tale

as I wait for the wintry sun to dapple
the caudal stain she left behind.

Song of the Northern Honeysuckle

Our vine pruned in September
some buds too high   just
leave them   let winter play
its staccato blast.

October frost   November freeze
overtop our trellis   yet Honeysuckle
clings to her hum-humble buds.

December nudges her song piano soft
as shy notes waft high into glissandos
          lilting far and wee.

What secret jingle
does Honey suckle?

Could be the blue sky blues   maybe baby.
No sleighs or reindeer   no *ho, ho, ho.*

Honey loves to sing   "The Holly and the Ivy"
loves solstice, wassail   "Auld Lang Syne."

Until a New Year sun kisses Honey's lips
mouths each bud open wide
          pollen arias rising.

Haiku Winter

Sunrays dazzle trees
White-frosted bushes twinkle
Flocks of sparrows hide

Snow skiffs on branches
Red berries dangle from limbs
Cedar waxwings feast

Brown-bodied squirrels
scurry up poplars to nest
safe from eagles' talons

Atop a bat box
heron eyes the pond below
Fish scales shimmery

Plowing through shallows
a cutthroat's dorsal fin swirls
hours from death's embrace

A mink swims to shore
swifts along the river's side
Silent fur silvers

Crawfish nestle mud
Huddles of legs and sharp claws
waking at sunset

Walking Down Sunday Roads

Winter at Robie Creek snow
crunches underfoot as you gaze

on high where ice crystals whirl
and evergreens spike a sapphire sky.

Elfin snowmen staggered by plows
melt away in the afternoon sun.

An old truck noses a red sports car
its broken windshield iced over

a burlap Farm Feed & Seed cover
spells comic relief but now

watch your step a hound
jerks to the length of his chain

howls bellows barks like hell
ghosting his Pliocene ancestor.

If you stop here show no fear
walk slowly watch for ice,

ice hiddden under a fresh white gown
you must save yourself from falling.

The Hope for Winter Storms

*because the threat of clouds hung heavy from what appeared to be heaven
but is actually atmosphere a promise a source of ...*

The hope for winter storms which will bring the snow that melts
into creeks that run into rivers and lakes to rest in reservoirs
created by dams that hold the water to feed the canals carrying
the water to furrows for plants to drink and produce the wheat
and potatoes by which we thrive,

the hope for water to fill the aquifers to be pumped into pipes for
sprinklers that fling the water like rain onto thirsty alfalfa and
corn that feed the animals we butcher and cook by which we've
grown strong,

the hope for water cycles to celebrate: sea water seeding the clouds
that bring relief as ice and rain fill the aquifers ready for wells to
pump water to store in cisterns, tanks or barrels, to be balanced
on the heads of women or hauled in jars lashed to donkeys or
carried in buckets, or flow from faucets,

for the world we know depends on water by which we calculate the
seasons, water poured into cups and glasses to slake our thirst,
water in our mouths

water by which we speak.

River Therapy

Webs of swooning capillaries
any of the fine branching streams
penetrating the flanks of mountains

water wraps swiftly surrounding the drop of a hat.
Melting snow shivers its banks the river's hunger mounts
gush of refusing confinement
flush as if her water broke

say this morning is the beginning of the world
who's to know it's not?

the Earth is another story
all solid, whirling through space
turning its rumtum body round
facing the sun

the sun that never fails
mornings the gnatcatchers' peeping
from the river mouth splits the air
a cracked plate sailing on oceanic seams.

I certify the crack in the plate
will have it notarized by noon.

How does nothing compare with nothing?
Or is absence the fulfillment of no thing?
Notice the corner where I kept the empties
floating on the river of misunderstanding.

Days pour forth like complaints
a need to travel upstream
search a mellow meadow
near 8th and sunflower?
but the morning saunters.

Water has no color
water is always hungry
settles into levels of kindly banks
where you may step into the river
be swept away into the kingdom
listen, skinned logs.

Name Me Four in One

The Stir:
I come   from shadows clutched   by shear white drifts
a changeling   astir in soaked seedbeds   as husks rot
seedlings swell   bulbs blossom   warm winds   coddle
thawing limbs   pummeled by rain

Thumbs of Bright Colors:
I bask in sunny heat   as thumbs of bright colors   thrust up
on rings of hot days   sap-formed buds   fill to fruited globes
succulent ears kernel   straw necks bend in praise

Bringing in the Sheaves:
I ride the cusp   sword arm ready to slay hunger's gaunt heart
his body bruised   tethered sheaves of golden hue   burdens
sweet to carry   with humble mien   obedient axe soon
splitting wood to fuel hearth fires

Nodding Off:
I slumber deep in weary dark   eyes fiercely closed   feigned rest
our dank locks lengthen   curls of withering blasts   whip grassy
rooftops   bare-bent forest branches   snare the unwary walkers
felling foolish travelers

The Exeter Book from the tenth century contains more than ninety
riddles personifying such items as animals and tools as well as the
sun, storm, and the ocean. They may be read as both concrete and
allegorical poems.

V. Season After Season

Consider   I was born before numbers   still I'm used   measure
for measure   in my one   I harness twelve   who ride the sun
and moon   my ways may seem eternal   but where I go
none can follow

Who am I?

River People

Water calls to all who lust for distant vistas
                        high mountain springs   inlet campsites
trails leading people upriver   to hunt   fish
                the river   a sanctuary   belonging to all.
The people of this continent paused
                        as strangers came—a few and then many
finding the fertile shores of rivers
                        passing through, then staying on.
Les bois! French trappers shouted, *une rivière!* to become the Boise.
                Exhausted from endless miles of desert
overjoyed to see a sinuous green line   signifying
                river!   to be storied in chants   scrolls   poems
such as I write   on account of the Boise.

> *River cuts a rocky channel*
> *Tumbles down valleys*

Long ago tribes of humans clans coming together
                Native American Viking Basque Scottish
worshipping the sun   moon   ancestors,   a savior
                voices rising from shores   lochs   monoliths.
Prayers for safety from wind and rain
                        for plentiful game   salmon   potatoes
giving thanks for rivers   rafts   sails.

And me   catching my breath   loving the river
                        never still   living in stream time
bearing the weight of inherited histories.

> *River inviting all to gather*
> *Plenty of fish and berries*

2.

Ask how the earliest tribes came here

crossing a land bridge
                 in boats hugging a coastline   on outriggers

sailing the open seas millennia ago
                to edge onto a continent to be named America.
Driven by drums of hunger   days   months   years
              generations of hunters   gatherers   foragers
always a return to riverbanks for shelter.

> *Rivers feed cottonwoods*
>   *Cover for ducks   geese   eagles*

Ask old Grandfather how it all began

Kenu weaves scenes of those times
            when water was all   a beaver   an otter
a muskrat   diving down   one after the other
           braves eager to find   lairs of fish   water-people
each chasing a beautiful water-girl   she darting away.
            Little muskrat scrapes the bottom
emerges with a ball of mud on his nose
            forms the earth under our feet
the Great Spirit Apeh nods.

> *Mountains rise from lava*
>   *Wind breathes air clean*

3.

Ask why more people came

Settlers trusting creation   from the firmament   a garden
                 now a riddle   famine-forced
islanders from the Hebrides   Eigg   Rum   Muck
           my people   sail the broad sea   witness sundogs
green flashes   God's power   manifest at sundown.
                     Cyrus and Mary from Jura
Duncan and Angus   head on out west
            vast "empty" spaces   a new Eden.
Prairie schooners   streams of wagons   rolling   rolling
             across desert plains   over mountains
rolling down to the Boise   hot springs   bubbles
             pools of warmth heated by magma
ready to ease the bodies of weary travelers.

            Snow falls on peaks
              Summer sun feeds the river

Here I was born   emerged from Adam's rib   a woman
             a willful daughter of Eve   aroused
to cherish all the Earth   sisters   brothers
            ready to defend   creeks   rapids   eddies   lakes
honor the rivers   Boise   Snake   Columbia   knowing
            how even the oldest river   flows new every day.

            Season after season
             . *Year after year*

4.

Ask what my forefathers didn't know

How once long ago Basinu'yu walked on two legs
            but he was vain   stuck out his tongue   hissed
when anyone smiled or acted friendly to him
    but the people banded together   gave him a medicine spell
now he slithers on his belly   not rude or too good-looking
            a serpent   winding   through fields and forests
denizen of gardens and graveyards.

Ask how the war broke out

Settlers on the Snake River Plain   usurpers of tribal lands
            supplanting Shoshone Sheepeater Bannock Lemhi
tribes who knew how Izapuh, the coyote-spirit, became
                        Nu'gant'na   flew with goose girl
soaring near the sun   looking down   only to see
            square plots of earth   grass eaten by plows
trees in rows   dams on tributaries   water caught in ponds
            water spilled onto fields   rivers running low.

Water spread across the desert
The cottonwoods weeping

5.

Soon the tribal people   the Newe   went hungry
                    soldiers barred the camas harvests
women banned from foraging
                    hunters ride home empty-handed.
Soon warriors arose   raided settlers   striking like wildfire
                  blood of the ancestors   blood of the families
blood-soaked soil   rivers running red.

                Rain pours down in heavy weather
                Rain washes blood into the earth

People sent by treaty to reservations   old ways dying
                  new settlements strung along rivers
the length of the Snake River Plain
                  Boiseans build homes on tribal burial grounds.

Still the Shoshone and Bannock return in summer
                to ~~Castle Rock Reserve~~   Chief Eagle Eye Reserve
                to ~~Quarry View Park~~   Eagle Rock Park
where drums and dancing raise the spirits of ancestors
                people recall   how at first   nothing but water
until little muskrat swam up
                  with a ball of mud on his nose.

6.

In early light   I yearn for open vistas   strap on boots
                            to hike the dusty foothills
climb up Eagle Rock Park   see
                            how sparkling   the river flows today
but when I blunder   into magpie nests
                            their swift attack   dive-bombing   screaming
blocks the trail   stranding me   while underfoot
                            amidst the chaparral   a snake   riled.

I hear the rattle before I see the coil
                            diamond scales   shimmer in scatters of light
deadly beauty reminds me   of a time when proud
                            Basinu'yu also walked on two legs

how petroglyphs witnessed   the seekers
                            generations passing   tribes followed by settlers
until now   I stand among the ancestors   to watch the Boise
                            stream like a sunrise   because even the oldest river
is new today   wending its way
                            to the ocean's broad confluence   because
the river bends   but doesn't break.   Always   the river.

Notes: Recent discovery of ancient footprints date human activity on
    the continent far earlier than previously believed. NPR 2021/9/24/10
Chief Eagle Eye Reserve and Eagle Rock Park are new names adopted by
    the Boise City Council in June 2019 to honor the tribal significance
    of the Boise Valley Indigenous People. The sites also protect ancestral
    burial grounds.
The poem "River People" draws from *When the Smoke Goes Straight Up:
    Grandfather's Stories*, retold by Donna E. Houtz McArthur, 2012. I am a
    member of the McArthur clan.

After the Water

First frost? Drive upriver   cross the dam   look down
the canyon blocked to capture snowmelt, tame floods
a concrete wall to rescue cities from drowning. But now

look around   you see dry foothills   wind-borne seeds
like dust, clinging to gray scrub; how best intentions fly.
October and Lucky Peak Lake drained for thirsty fields

twenty-five hundred square miles of water nearly gone
used up   spent   like the wages of sin   like progress
where God knows no talents   are hidden under bushels.

Hike   hundreds of feet down   skitter the dry slope
muscles   cartilage   tendons   ankles   struggle
heels dig   slip   slide   into chances of dust to dust.

Now in the big empty   stop   listen   call out   echo
echo   then silence   only a   *ssshhhhh*   a sand delta
glissades   from parched canyon walls.

The season of thirst   stranded docks   withered mud
a lament peeling the lake bottom   sun-dried   curled
polygon skins underfoot   step/crunch   step/crunch

the dry   arid   fear of drought   threat of famine
crops blistered   like old skin on the faces of fields
the dry   not the thing itself   but roaming   like fear

like hunger   like herons   staring into pools where carp
lie trapped   breathing their last   as the sun takes its due
and you look up to the big sky. And what you see

is what you see   or do you see what's not there?
Because in the beginning   pioneers   read handbills
heard the word of mouth   like a whisper from God

rain can be trained   rain will follow the plow   come—
and the multitudes came   hearing the word of what was not
would never be—only desert rain   a devil's playground

salmon   native lifestyles   people   damned by progress
ditches like veins   prayers for snow.   Destiny they said.
Now climb out of the canyon   look back   twelve miles

of big empty   then sky—and settle into a lawn chair
wait for sunset   dark   when Orionid meteors shower fire.
Or Halley's Comet bows to the sharp white of a Hunter Moon.

Winter Wings

The day I soared   the sky cloud-frowned   unfallen snow   and what
was there?   Wings aloft   an air-born stream   a blossoming dress
rehearsal   a choir of windblown angels.   I lifted my eyes to see

the lean heron fold and unfold its everlasting arms slate without
weight pterodactyl complement to firmament. Or now, see?
Dozens and dozens of chickadee sprites a flock dressed in cubist-
conformity bursting from treetops *zip! zip!* O, do you hear? the
Celtic faerie's *dee-dee-dee.*

Listen, please as I recall the first freeze, the frost. Our little dogwood
tipped with bouncy, bitter berries until the nip of it red rounds
sun-warmed suddenly succulent. Flickers cling from branch to
twig their black bibs first in line beaks primed *peck, peck.* Then the
squirrels.

On into December's darkest clime how birds survive messengers
of light defying wind gusts blow after blow icy finger-spikes to
feathered foreheads and still solstice flies by night lightens the
earth while I come to you moment by moment arms lifted days
lengthening

and I believe so
for I have flown in splendor
one day and the next.

December Moon

With silence like absence, you rise
peeking above rooftops and further
to shimmer the backs of black branches
silhouetted treetops stretched in disarray
to my eye, speaking their woody lines
your beams whitening the white snow
that does not move or reflect
but rather absorbs your cold rays
the ones reaching down to touch my hand
briefly dusted by the shadow of a great owl
in search of a scampering mouse
to shimmer the backs of branches
hoo-h'HOO-hoo-hoo
we three signatories to the future

and this is the question, the who
of our years passing into a calendar,
days slipping away whether or not
anyone hears the owl's voice, or yours
or mine, speaking of our ages and what
we've learned or have yet to
before crossing into moonlight
the invisible once and still poised.

Title Index

T

W

Z

First Line Index

9 781594 981289